GOD'S RAINBOW OF PROMISES

GOD'S RAINBOW OF PROMISES

All rights reserved
Copyright © 1984 Ernest Angley
Printed in the United States of America
Distributed by Winston Press,
P.O. Box 2091, Akron, Ohio 44309.
ISBN 0-9636772-1-7

"Whereby are given unto us exceeding great and precious promises: that by these ye might be partakers of the divine nature . . ."

II Peter 1:4

CONTENTS

Introduction by Reverend Ernest Angley

Chapter 1. God is Faithful

Chapter 2. The Key to Receiving: Faith and Obedience

Chapter 3. Prayer and Fasting

Chapter 4. Salvation and Eternal Life

Chapter 5. The Holy Ghost Baptism

Chapter 6. Spiritual Growth

Chapter 7. The Rapture

Chapter 8. Physical Healing

Chapter 9. Protection From and Victory Over Satan

Chapter 10. Abundant Life

Chapter 11. Financial and Material Blessings

Chapter 12. Guidance and a Plain Path

Chapter 13. Help in Time of Need

A Final Word of Encouragement

INTRODUCTION

Dear Reader,

Every one of God's promises are sincerely given to all humanity. He carefully watches over those promises with His all-seeing eyes so that they are fulfilled for God-fearing, God-loving people who dare to walk holy all the time with Christ the Son of God dwelling inside them by the power of the Holy Ghost.

In Eden, man and woman did not live on the promises of God. They had living reality of God, and all His greatness was theirs; no promises were needed—everything was given without promise. All was provided to give man and woman perfect days.

Outside Eden, man and woman must live on the promises of God. They must show trust in what God has said and prove they want Him and His help.

God gave Noah a fantastic Rainbow of Promise after the flood. Thousands of years have passed, and that Rainbow of Promise has been kept. God has displayed the rainbow again and again to all generations to remind humanity that He made a promise which was to include the entire human race, and He has kept that promise, reminding us that all His promises are Rainbow Promises. All the love, faithfulness and strength of Lord God Almighty used in keeping the Noah Rainbow Promise is used to keep each and every Rainbow

Promise made to the human race.

It was impossible to gather all the Rainbow Promises for you today, but I have tried to gather in one basket enough of the Rainbow Promises from God to cover every need you have or will ever have. Humbly, I present to you a basket full of God's Rainbow Promises fresh from heaven, just as fresh as if God had spoken them today.

We must allow His strength to flow through us from His promises of power, help and deliverance. Reach into the basket with God's faith and love daily for all things needed.

Yours standing on His promises,

Ernest Angley

Reverend Ernest Angley

1
God Is Faithful

The Lord has provided a rainbow of many marvelous promises in His Word. He will always keep His promises. The only one who can hinder you in receiving from God's Rainbow of Promises is you yourself, for God is faithful who promised. But the promises of God are conditional.

Know therefore that the Lord thy God, he is God, the faithful God, which keepeth covenant and mercy with them that love him and keep his commandments to a thousand generations *(Deuteronomy 7:9)*.

For I am the Lord, I change not *(Malachi 3:6)*.

Jesus Christ the same yesterday, and to-day, and for ever *(Hebrews 13:8)*.

Let us hold fast the profession of our faith without wavering; (for he is faithful that promised) *(Hebrews 10:23)*.

So shall my word be that goeth forth out of my mouth: it shall not return unto me void, but it shall accomplish that which I please, and it shall prosper in the thing whereto I sent it *(Isaiah 55:11)*.

But the Lord is faithful, who shall stablish you, and keep you from evil *(II Thessalonians 3:3)*.

God is faithful, by whom ye were called unto the fellowship of his Son Jesus Christ our Lord *(I Corinthians 1:9)*.

There hath not failed one word of all his good promise *(I Kings 8:56)*.

If we believe not, yet he abideth faithful: he cannot deny himself *(II Timothy 2:13)*.

And being fully persuaded that, what he had promised, he was able also to perform *(Romans 4:21)*.

For all the promises of God in him are yea, and in him Amen, unto the glory of God by us *(II Corinthians 1:20)*.

Thy mercy, O Lord, is in the heavens; and thy faithfulness reacheth unto the clouds *(Psalm 36:5)*.

The eternal God is thy refuge, and underneath are the everlasting arms *(Deuteronomy 33:27)*.

That by two immutable things, in which it was impossible for God to lie, we might have a strong consolation, who have fled for refuge to lay hold upon the hope set before us *(Hebrews 6:18)*.

Heaven and earth shall pass away: but my words shall not pass away *(Mark 13:31)*.

But the mercy of the Lord is from everlasting to everlasting upon them that fear him, and his righteousness unto children's children *(Psalm 103:17)*.

As for God, his way is perfect: the word of the Lord is tried: he is a buckler to all those that trust in him *(Psalm 18:30)*.

2
The Key To Receiving: Faith and Obedience

Do not be afraid to ask something great of the Lord. Why hesitate to stake your claim when God's Rainbow of Promises gives you that right? The Bible tells us that nothing is impossible with God; He can do anything—and He will—for those who trust and obey.

For what if some did not believe? shall their unbelief make the faith of God without effect? God forbid: yea, let God be true, but every man a liar *(Romans 3:3,4).*

Trust in the Lord with all thine heart; and lean not unto thine own understanding. In all thy ways acknowledge him, and he shall direct thy paths *(Proverbs 3:5,6).*

Now faith is the substance of things hoped for, the evidence of things not seen *(Hebrews 11:1).*

God hath dealt to every man the measure of faith *(Romans 12:3).*

Faith cometh by hearing . . . the word of God *(Romans 10:17).*

If ye keep my commandments, ye shall abide in my love; even as I have kept my Father's commandments, and abide in his love *(John 15:10).*

Now therefore, if ye will obey my voice indeed, and keep my covenant, then ye shall be a peculiar treasure unto me *(Exodus 19:5).*

And let us not be weary in well-doing: for in due season we shall reap, if we faint not *(Galatians 6:9).*

But the mercy of the Lord is from everlasting to everlasting upon them that fear him, and his righteousness unto children's children; To such as keep his covenant, and to those that remember his commandments to do them *(Psalm 103:17,18)*.

If thou canst believe, all things are possible to him that believeth *(Mark 9:23)*.

Behold, I am the Lord, the God of all flesh: is there anything too hard for me *(Jeremiah 32:27)?*

Now the just shall live by faith *(Hebrews 10:38)*.

The Lord is my light and my salvation; whom shall I fear? the Lord is the strength of my life; of whom shall I be afraid *(Psalm 27:1)?*

Believe in the Lord your God, so shall ye be established; believe his prophets, so shall ye prosper *(II Chronicles 20:20)*.

But without faith it is impossible to please him; for he that cometh to God must believe that he is, and that he is a rewarder of them that diligently seek him *(Hebrews 11:6)*.

Ask in faith, nothing wavering. For he that wavereth is like a wave of the sea driven with the wind and tossed. For let not that man think that he shall receive any thing of the Lord *(James 1:6,7)*.

If ye have faith as a grain of mustard seed, ye shall say unto this mountain, Remove hence to yonder place; and it shall remove; and nothing shall be impossible unto you *(Matthew 17:20)*.

According to your faith be it unto you *(Matthew 9:29)*.

Trust in the Lord, and do good; so shalt thou dwell in the land, and verily thou shalt be fed *(Psalm 37:3).*

Commit thy way unto the Lord; trust also in him; and he shall bring it to pass *(Psalm 37:5).*

They that trust in the Lord shall be as mount Zion, which cannot be removed, but abideth for ever *(Psalm 125:1).*

This book of the law shall not depart out of thy mouth; but thou shalt meditate therein day and night, that thou mayest observe to do according to all that is written therein: for then thou shalt make thy way prosperous, and then thou shalt have good success *(Joshua 1:8).*

Cast not away therefore your confidence, which hath great recompense of reward. For ye have need of patience, that, after ye have done the will of God, ye might receive the promise *(Hebrews 10:35, 36).*

And thou shalt love the Lord thy God with all thine heart, and with all thy soul, and with all thy might *(Deuteronomy 6:5).*

If they obey and serve him, they shall spend their days in prosperity, and their years in pleasures *(Job 36:11).*

If ye be willing and obedient, ye shall eat the good of the land *(Isaiah 1:19).*

3
God's Promises Concerning Prayer and Fasting

Prayer and fasting are included in God's Rainbow of Promises; in fact, some promises cannot be claimed merely by prayer, but by prayer *and* fasting. Fasting is a condition for some miracles. Jesus fasted forty days; Paul spent much time in prayer and fasting. Even when these conditions are met, some Christians still allow themselves to be cheated out of what God offers because they look to the doubt that the devil brings rather than to the promises of God. Faith wavers and the promises go unclaimed.

When you pray, ask in faith, nothing wavering (James 1:6). Pray, fast, fix your eyes on the Lord, looking neither to the right nor to the left as you claim the abundance God has promised you in His Rainbow of Promises.

Therefore I say unto you, What things soever ye desire, when ye pray, believe that ye receive them, and ye shall have them *(Mark 11:24)*.

Ask, and it shall be given you; seek, and ye shall find; knock, and it shall be opened unto you: For every one that asketh receiveth; and he that seeketh findeth; and to him that knocketh it shall be opened . . . If ye then, being evil, know how to give good gifts unto your children, how much more shall your Father which is in heaven give good things to them that ask him *(Matthew 7:7,8,11)?*

Is not this the fast that I have chosen? to loose the bands of wickedness, to undo the heavy burdens, and to let the oppressed go free, and that ye break every yoke? . . . Then shalt thou call, and the Lord shall answer; thou shalt cry, and he shall say, Here I am . . . And the Lord shall guide thee continually *(Isaiah 58:6,9,11)*.

If ye abide in me, and my words abide in you, ye shall ask what ye will, and it shall be done unto you *(John 15:7)*.

And this is the confidence that we have in him, that, if we ask any thing according to his will, he heareth us: And if we know that he hear us, whatsoever we ask, we know that we have the petitions that we desired of him *(I John 5:14,15)*.

Howbeit this kind goeth not out but by prayer and fasting *(Matthew 17:21)*.

And call upon me in the day of trouble: I will deliver thee, and thou shalt glorify me *(Psalm 50:15).*

For the eyes of the Lord are over the righteous, and his ears are open unto their prayers *(I Peter 3:12).*

Draw nigh to God, and he will draw nigh to you *(James 4:8).*

Again I say unto you, That if two of you shall agree on earth as touching any thing that they shall ask, it shall be done for them of my Father which is in heaven *(Matthew 18:19).*

For where two or three are gathered together in my name, there am I in the midst of them *(Matthew 18:20).*

Watch and pray, that ye enter not into temptation: the spirit indeed is willing, but the flesh is weak *(Matthew 26:41).*

And he spake a parable unto them to this end, that men ought always to pray, and not to faint *(Luke 18:1).*

Hitherto have ye asked nothing in my name: ask, and ye shall receive, that your joy may be full *(John 16:24).*

Is any among you afflicted? let him pray . . . *(James 5:13).*

He shall call upon me, and I will answer him: I will be with him in trouble; I will deliver him, and honour him *(Psalm 91:15).*

And it shall come to pass, that before they call, I will answer; and while they are yet speaking, I will hear *(Isaiah 65:24).*

If my people, which are called by my name, shall humble themselves, and pray, and seek my face, and turn from their wicked ways; then will I hear from heaven, and will forgive their sin, and will heal their land *(II Chronicles 7:14).*

And ye shall seek me, and find me, when ye shall search for me with all your heart *(Jeremiah 29:13).*

Confess your faults one to another, and pray one for another, that ye may be healed. The effectual fervent prayer of a righteous man availeth much *(James 5:16).*

And whatsoever we ask, we receive of him, because we keep his commandments, and do those things that are pleasing in his sight *(I John 3:22).*

I love them that love me; and those that seek me early shall find me *(Proverbs 8:17).*

Then I proclaimed a fast there, at the river of Ahava, that we might afflict ourselves before our God, to seek of him a right way for us, and for our little ones, and for all our substance. So we fasted and besought our God for this: and he was entreated of us *(Ezra 8:21,23).*

But thou, when thou fastest, anoint thine head, and wash thy face; That thou appear not unto men to fast, but unto thy Father which is in secret: and thy Father, which seeth in secret, shall reward thee openly *(Matthew 6:17,18).*

And . . . he [Jesus] . . . fasted forty days and forty nights *(Matthew 4:2).*

Defraud ye not one the other, except it be with consent for a time, that ye may give yourselves to fasting and prayer *(I Corinthians 7:5).*

4

God's Promises Concerning Salvation and Eternal Life

Jesus came to earth and paid a great price to set up the plan of redemption for all mankind, a Rainbow Promise sealed with His precious blood. Jesus gave all that we might have all. What are we redeemed from? Our sin nature that would send us to hell when we die.

Jesus warns of the reality of hell—a place many try to convince themselves is not there—and the Bible clearly talks about hell and its reality: *The wicked shall be turned into hell, and all the nations that forget God* (Psalm 9:17); *[Hell] where their worm [soul] dieth not, and the fire is not quenched* (Mark 9:48); *And in hell he [the rich man] lift up his eyes, being in torments* (Luke 16:23).

There is a literal, burning hell; it is not just a state of mind. If there were no hell, it would not have been necessary for Jesus to have come to earth and to have suffered so horribly on the cross so that mankind could escape eternal damnation. The promise of heaven in the Rainbow of Promises is conditional; not everyone will go there. Not everyone will meet the requirements, although it is possible for all to do so. As Jesus told Nicodemus: You must be born again.

For God so loved the world, that he gave his only begotten Son, that whosoever believeth in him should not perish, but have everlasting life *(John 3:16).*

For all have sinned, and come short of the glory of God; Being justified freely by his grace through the redemption that is in Christ Jesus: Whom God hath set forth to be a propitiation THROUGH FAITH IN HIS BLOOD, to declare his righteousness for the remission of sins that are past *(Romans 3:23-25).*

For by grace are ye saved through faith; and that not of yourselves; it is the gift of God *(Ephesians 2:8).*

Except a man be born again, he cannot see the kingdom of God *(John 3:3).*

That if thou shalt confess with thy mouth the Lord Jesus, and shalt believe in thine heart that God hath raised him from the dead, thou shalt be saved *(Romans 10:9).*

But if we walk in the light, as he is in the light, we have fellowship one with another, and the blood of Jesus Christ his Son cleanseth us from all sin *(I John 1:7).*

In my Father's house are many mansions: if it were not so, I would have told you. I go to prepare a place for you. And if I go and prepare a place for you, I will come again, and receive you unto myself; that where I am, there ye may be also *(John 14:2,3).*

And this is the promise that he hath promised us, even eternal life *(I John 2:25).*

And this is the record, that God hath given to us eternal life, and this life is in his Son. He that hath the Son hath life; and he that hath not the Son of God hath not life *(I John 5:11,12)*.

Neither is there salvation in any other: for there is none other name under heaven given among men, whereby we must be saved *(Acts 4:12)*.

If we confess our sins, he is faithful and just to forgive us our sins, and to cleanse us from all unrighteousness *(I John 1:9)*.

Therefore if any man be in Christ, he is a new creature: old things are passed away; behold, all things are become new *(II Corinthians 5:17)*.

There is therefore now no condemnation to them which are in Christ Jesus, who walk not after the flesh, but after the Spirit. For the law of the Spirit of life in Christ Jesus hath made me free from the law of sin and death *(Romans 8:1,2)*.

[God] who will have all men to be saved, and to come unto the knowledge of the truth *(I Timothy 2:4)*.

For the grace of God that bringeth salvation hath appeared to all men *(Titus 2:11)*.

Whosoever shall call on the name of the Lord shall be saved *(Acts 2:21)*.

Therefore as by the offence of one judgment came

upon all men to condemnation; even so by the righteousness of one the free gift came upon all men unto justification of life *(Romans 5:18).*

But the salvation of the righteous is of the Lord *(Psalm 37:39).*

Behold, I was shapen in iniquity, and in sin did my mother conceive me . . . Purge me with hyssop, and I shall be clean: wash me, and I shall be whiter than snow . . . Hide thy face from my sins, and blot out all mine iniquities. Create in me a clean heart, O God; and renew a right spirit within me *(Psalm 51:5,7,9,10).*

Come now, and let us reason together, saith the Lord: though your sins be as scarlet, they shall be as white as snow; though they be red like crimson, they shall be as wool *(Isaiah 1:18).*

And ye shall seek me, and find me, when ye shall search for me with all your heart *(Jeremiah 29:13).*

Seek ye the Lord while he may be found, call ye upon him while he is near: Let the wicked forsake his way, and the unrighteous man his thoughts: and let him return unto the Lord, and he will have mercy upon him; and to our God, for he will abundantly pardon *(Isaiah 55:6,7).*

I am crucified with Christ: nevertheless I live; yet not I, but Christ liveth in me: and the life which I now live in the flesh I live by the faith of the Son of God, who loved me, and gave himself for me *(Galatians 2:20).*

But we believe that through the grace of the Lord Jesus Christ we shall be saved *(Acts 15:11)*.

I am the door; by me if any man enter in, he shall be saved *(John 10:9)*.

For God hath not appointed us to wrath, but to obtain salvation by our Lord Jesus Christ *(I Thessalonians 5:9)*.

For whosoever shall call upon the name of the Lord shall be saved *(Romans 10:13)*.

For the wages of sin is death; but the gift of God is eternal life through Jesus Christ our Lord *(Romans 6:23)*.

But God commendeth his love toward us, in that, while we were yet sinners, Christ died for us. Much more then, being now justified by his blood, we shall be saved from wrath through him *(Romans 5:8,9)*.

These things have I written unto you that believe on the name of the Son of God; that ye may know that ye have eternal life, and that ye may believe on the name of the Son of God *(I John 5:13)*.

There is no man that hath left house, or parents, or brethren, or wife, or children, for the kingdom of God's sake, Who shall not receive manifold more in this present time, and in the world to come life everlasting *(Luke 18:29,30)*.

For he that soweth to his flesh shall of the flesh reap

corruption; but he that soweth to the Spirit shall of the Spirit reap life everlasting *(Galatians 6:8).*

But the righteous hath hope in his death *(Proverbs 14:32).*

Which hope we have as an anchor of the soul, both sure and steadfast *(Hebrews 6:19).*

For I reckon that the sufferings of this present time are not worthy to be compared with the glory which shall be revealed in us *(Romans 8:18).*

But lay up for yourselves treasures in heaven, where neither moth nor rust doth corrupt, and where thieves do not break through nor steal *(Matthew 6:20).*

The holy scriptures, which are able to make thee wise unto salvation through faith which is in Christ Jesus *(II Timothy 3:15).*

Because it is written, Be ye holy; for I am holy . . . Forasmuch as ye know that ye were not redeemed with corruptible things, as silver and gold . . . But with the precious blood of Christ, as of a lamb without blemish and without spot *(I Peter 1:16,18,19).*

As Christ was raised up from the dead by the glory of the Father, even so we also should walk in newness of life *(Romans 6:4).*

Verily, verily, I say unto you, He that heareth my word, and believeth on him that sent me, hath everlasting life, and shall not come into condemnation;

but is passed from death unto life *(John 5:24)*.

And if any man sin, we have an advocate with the Father, Jesus Christ the righteous: And he is the propitiation for our sins: and not for our's only, but also for the sins of the whole world *(I John 2:1,2)*.

For sin shall not have dominion over you *(Romans 6:14)*.

For we know that, if our earthly house of this tabernacle were dissolved, we have a building of God, an house not made with hands, eternal in the heavens *(II Corinthians 5:1)*.

Blessed are they that do his commandments, that they may have right to the tree of life, and may enter in through the gates into the city *(Revelation 22:14)*.

And they that be wise shall shine as the brightness of the firmament; and they that turn many to righteousness as the stars for ever and ever *(Daniel 12:3)*.

To him that overcometh will I grant to sit with me in my throne, even as I also overcame, and am set down with my Father in his throne *(Revelation 3:21)*.

I, even I, am he that blotteth out thy transgressions for mine own sake, and will not remember thy sins *(Isaiah 43:25)*.

5
God's Promises Concerning the Holy Ghost Baptism

After you have received the promise of salvation, what is next? Receiving the promise of the blessed Holy Ghost—not only a privilege but also a command of Jesus—a vital part of God's Rainbow of Promises. It's an experience separate from the experience of salvation. The baptism in the Holy Ghost, with its initial evidence of speaking in tongues, is a condition that must be met if you expect to be changed in a moment, in a twinkling of an eye, at the second coming of Jesus, the Rapture of the Church. It will take the baptism in the Holy Ghost to adequately prepare you for the Rapture.

Have ye received the Holy Ghost since ye believed? And when Paul had laid his hands upon them, the Holy Ghost came on them; and they spake with tongues, and prophesied *(Acts 19:2,6).*

Then laid they their hands on them, and they received the Holy Ghost *(Acts 8:17).*

[Jesus] being assembled together with them, COMMANDED them that they should not depart from Jerusalem, but wait for the promise of the Father . . . For John truly baptized with water; but ye shall be baptized with the Holy Ghost not many days hence *(Acts 1:4,5).*

For he [the Holy Spirit] dwelleth with you, and shall be in you *(John 14:17).*

And when the day of Pentecost was fully come . . . they were all filled with the Holy Ghost, and began to speak with other tongues, as the Spirit gave them utterance *(Acts 2:1,4).*

I indeed baptize you with water unto repentance: but he that cometh after me is mightier than I, whose shoes I am not worthy to bear: he shall baptize you with the Holy Ghost, and with fire *(Matthew 3:11).*

For the promise is unto you, and to your children, and to all that are afar off, even as many as the Lord our God shall call *(Acts 2:39).*

But the Comforter, which is the Holy Ghost, whom the Father will send in my name, he shall teach you all things and bring all things to your remembrance, whatsoever I have said unto you *(John 14:26)*.

Howbeit when he, the Spirit of truth, is come, he will guide you into all truth . . . he will shew you things to come *(John 16:13)*.

But ye shall receive power, after that the Holy Ghost is come upon you: and ye shall be witnesses unto me *(Acts 1:8)*.

Likewise the Spirit also helpeth our infirmities: for we know not what we should pray for as we ought: but the Spirit itself maketh intercession for us with groanings which cannot be uttered. And he that searcheth the hearts knoweth what is the mind of the Spirit, because he maketh intercession for the saints according to the will of God *(Romans 8:26,27)*.

And it shall come to pass afterward, that I will pour out my Spirit upon all flesh; and your sons and your daughters shall prophesy, your old men shall dream dreams, your young men shall see visions *(Joel 2:28)*.

If ye then, being evil, know how to give good gifts unto your children: how much more shall your heavenly Father give the Holy Spirit to them that ask him? *(Luke 11:13)*.

And, behold, I send the promise of my Father upon you: but tarry ye in the city of Jerusalem, until ye be endued with power from on high *(Luke 24:49)*.

Repent, and be baptized every one of you in the name

of Jesus Christ for the remission of sins, and ye shall receive the gift of the Holy Ghost *(Acts 2:38)*.

For the Holy Ghost shall teach you in the same hour what ye ought to say *(Luke 12:12)*.

Which things also we speak, not in the words which man's wisdom teacheth, but which the Holy Ghost teacheth; comparing spiritual things with spiritual *(I Corinthians 2:13)*.

And these signs shall follow them that believe ... they shall speak with new tongues *(Mark 16:17)*.

And I will pray the Father, and he shall give you another Comforter, that he may abide with you for ever *(John 14:16)*.

6
God's Promises Concerning Spiritual Growth

Some have never sought God, nor grown in Him spiritually; they expect life to always maintain its calm status quo. Sitting outside a dead church like the four starving lepers sat outside the gate of a besieged city, some Christians fail to reach for the benefits in God's Rainbow of Promises; and, consequently, those benefits remain unused. One day, however, the lepers said to themselves: *Why sit we here until we die?* They rose up and went to the camp of the enemy, finding the enemy had fled and left behind plentiful food and possessions.

Why sit you in the same spiritual rut until you die? Move on into the deeper things of the Lord. Astounding richness, marvelous things are contained in God's Rainbow of Promises. Although the promises are freely given to all by Jesus Christ, you must be diligent to claim them as you press onward toward the great prize and the secret place of the Most High.

Whereby are given unto us exceeding great and precious promises: that by these ye might be partakers of the divine nature *(II Peter 1:4)*.

Abide in me, and I in you. As the branch cannot bear fruit of itself, except it abide in the vine; no more can ye, except ye abide in me. I am the vine, ye are the branches: He that abideth in me, and I in him, the same bringeth forth much fruit: for without me ye can do nothing *(John 15:4,5)*.

But the fruit of the Spirit is love, joy, peace, longsuffering, gentleness, goodness, faith, Meekness, temperance *(Galatians 5:22,23)*.

As newborn babes, desire the sincere milk of the word, that ye may grow thereby *(I Peter 2:2)*.

Not as though I had already attained, either were already perfect: but I follow after, if that I may apprehend that for which also I am apprehended of Christ Jesus *(Philippians 3:12)*.

For in him dwelleth all the fulness of the Godhead bodily. And ye are complete in him *(Colossians 2:9,10)*.

But whoso keepeth his word, in him verily is the love of God perfected: hereby know we that we are in him *(I John 2:5)*.

For he satisfieth the longing soul, and filleth the hungry soul with goodness *(Psalm 107:9)*.

Now he which stablisheth us with you in Christ, and hath anointed us, is God *(II Corinthians 1:21).*

And be not conformed to this world: but be ye transformed by the renewing of your mind *(Romans 12:2).*

But he that received seed into the good ground is he that heareth the word, and understandeth it; which also beareth fruit, and bringeth forth, some an hundredfold, some sixty, some thirty *(Matthew 13:23).*

Wherefore, my brethren, ye also are become dead to the law by the body of Christ; that ye should be married to another, even to him who is raised from the dead, that we should bring forth fruit unto God *(Romans 7:4).*

Blessed is the man that walketh not in the counsel of the ungodly, nor standeth in the way of sinners, nor sitteth in the seat of the scornful. But his delight is in the law of the Lord; and in his law doth he meditate day and night. And he shall be like a tree planted by the rivers of water, that bringeth forth his fruit in his season; his leaf also shall not wither; and whatsoever he doeth shall prosper *(Psalm 1:1-3).*

Man doth not live by bread only, but by every word that proceedeth out of the mouth of the Lord doth man live *(Deuteronomy 8:3).*

God is my strength and power: And he maketh my way perfect *(II Samuel 22:33).*

I in them, and thou in me, that they may be made perfect in one; and that the world may know that thou hast sent me, and hast loved them, as thou hast loved me *(John 17:23).*

[Now the God of peace] make you perfect in every good work to do his will, working in you that which is well-pleasing in his sight, through Jesus Christ *(Hebrews 13:21).*

But we all, with open face beholding as in a glass the glory of the Lord, are changed into the same image from glory to glory, even as by the Spirit of the Lord *(II Corinthians 3:18).*

And Jesus said unto them, I am the bread of life: he that cometh to me shall never hunger; and he that believeth on me shall never thirst *(John 6:35).*

7
God's Promises Concerning the Rapture

The great pouring out of the Spirit has begun, and it will culminate with the return of Jesus as He comes to claim those who have been faithful and obedient to the Word of God. The generation is now upon the face of the earth that will see the coming of the Lord. The Rapture is an essential part of God's Rainbow of Promises.

We which are alive and remain unto the coming of the Lord shall not prevent them which are asleep. For the Lord himself shall descend from heaven with a shout, with the voice of the archangel, and with the trump of God: and the dead in Christ shall rise first: Then we which are alive and remain shall be caught up together with them in the clouds, to meet the Lord in the air: and so shall we ever be with the Lord *(I Thessalonians 4:15-17).*

This same Jesus, which is taken up from you into heaven, shall so come in like manner as ye have seen him go into heaven *(Acts 1:11).*

I will come again, and receive you unto myself; that where I am, there ye may be also *(John 14:3).*

Looking for that blessed hope, and the glorious appearing of the great God and our Saviour Jesus Christ *(Titus 2:13).*

And now, little children, abide in him; that, when he shall appear, we may have confidence, and not be ashamed before him at his coming *(I John 2:28).*

Watch therefore: for ye know not what hour your Lord doth come . . . Therefore be ye also ready: for in such an hour as ye think not the Son of man cometh *(Matthew 24:42,44).*

We look for the Saviour, the Lord Jesus Christ: Who shall change our vile body, that it may be fashioned like unto his glorious body *(Philippians 3:20,21).*

When Christ, who is our life, shall appear, then shall ye also appear with him in glory *(Colossians 3:4).*

Beloved, now are we the sons of God, and it doth not yet appear what we shall be: but we know that, when he shall appear, we shall be like him; for we shall see him as he is *(I John 3:2).*

And at midnight there was a cry made, Behold, the bridegroom cometh; go ye out to meet him . . . and they that were ready went in with him to the marriage: and the door was shut *(Matthew 25:6,10).*

Because thou hast kept the word of my patience, I also will keep thee from the hour of temptation, which shall come upon all the world, to try them that dwell upon the earth *(Revelation 3:10).*

For as the lightning cometh out of the east, and shineth even unto the west; so shall also the coming of the Son of man be *(Matthew 24:27).*

But as the days of Noe were, so shall also the coming of the Son of man be. For as in the days that were before the flood they were eating and drinking, marrying and giving in marriage, until the day that Noe entered into the ark *(Matthew 24:37,38).*

8
God's Promises Concerning Physical Healing

Jesus declared in His Word that healing is the children's bread—on the table with every meal. When doctors have no more control over your case, God has. The Bible states that Jesus is the same yesterday, today and forever; this means He will heal today and in the future because He healed yesterday. Healing is promised to all in the Word of God, but it's a promise that must be claimed; it is conditional. It is God's will for all to be healed. Jesus has provided healing in the atonement: *With His stripes we are healed* (Isaiah 53:5). Why not take advantage of God's Rainbow of Promises and receive this marvelous provision of healing He has made available to you?

But he was wounded for our transgressions, he was bruised for our iniquities: the chastisement of our peace was upon him; and with his stripes we are healed *(Isaiah 53:5)*.

[Christ] who his own self bare our sins in his own body on the tree, that we, being dead to sins, should live unto righteousness: by whose stripes ye were healed *(I Peter 2:24)*.

The Spirit of the Lord is upon me, because he hath anointed me to preach the gospel to the poor; he hath sent me to heal the brokenhearted, to preach deliverance to the captives, and recovering of sight to the blind, to set at liberty them that are bruised *(Luke 4:8)*.

And these signs shall follow them that believe; In my name . . . they shall lay hands on the sick, and they shall recover *(Mark 16:17,18)*.

Now concerning spiritual gifts, brethren, I would not have you ignorant . . . For to one is given . . . the gifts of healing by the same Spirit; To another the working of miracles *(I Corinthians 12:1,8-10)*.

I will take sickness away from the midst of thee *(Exodus 23:25)*.

And the Lord will take away from thee all sickness *(Deuteronomy 7:15)*.

Neither shall any plague come nigh thy dwelling *(Psalm 91:10)*.

[The Lord] who healeth all thy diseases *(Psalm 103:3).*

He sent his word, and healed them *(Psalm 107:20).*

But unto you that fear my name shall the Sun of righteousness arise with healing in his wings *(Malachi 4:2).*

Beloved, I wish above all things that thou mayest prosper and be in health, even as thy soul prospereth *(III John 2).*

Verily, verily, I say unto you, He that believeth on me, the works that I do shall he do also; and greater works than these shall he do; because I go unto my Father *(John 14:12).*

Is any sick among you? let him call for the elders of the church; and let them pray over him, anointing him with oil in the name of the Lord: And the prayer of faith shall save the sick, and the Lord shall raise him up *(James 5:14,15).*

Every good gift and every perfect gift is from above, and cometh down from the Father *(James 1:17).*

If thou wilt diligently hearken to the voice of the Lord thy God, and wilt do that which is right in his sight, and wilt give ear to his commandments, and keep all his statutes, I will put none of these diseases upon thee, which I have brought upon the Egyptians: for I am the Lord that healeth thee *(Exodus 15:26).*

And God wrought special miracles by the hands of Paul: So that from his body were brought unto the sick handkerchiefs or aprons, and the diseases departed from them, and the evil spirits went out of them *(Acts 19:11,12).*

9
God's Promises Concerning Protection From and Victory Over Satan

David was a young man who met the Lord's qualifications and obligations. Not another Israelite had been willing to face the fearsome giant Goliath until David came with the overcoming power of the Lord and this challenge: *Who is this uncircumcised Philistine that he should defy the armies of the living God?* David knew how to put his faith in God for the impossible, for victory over the enemy. He reached into God's Rainbow of Promises with an obedient heart, nothing doubting; David was obedience and trust in action, and God brought the victory.

The Apostle Paul is another example of one who drew upon God's Rainbow of Promises with perfect trust and obedience. Although he came face to face with much adversity—beaten, shipwrecked, stoned and left for dead, imprisoned—throughout his walk with the Lord, God always enabled him to triumph in Christ Jesus. He left us with this testimony: *Who shall separate us from the love of Christ? shall tribulation, or distress, or persecution, or famine, or nakedness, or peril, or sword?. . . Nay, in all these things we are more than conquerors through him that loved us. For I am persuaded, that neither death, nor life, nor angels, nor principalities, nor powers, nor things present, nor things to come, Nor height, nor depth, nor any other creature, shall be able to separate us from the love of God, which is in Christ Jesus our Lord* (Romans 8:35,37-39).

Put on the whole armour of God, that ye may be able to stand against the wiles of the devil. For we wrestle not against flesh and blood, but against principalities, against powers, against the rulers of the darkness of this world, against spiritual wickedness in high places. Wherefore take unto you the whole armour of God, that ye may be able to withstand in the evil day, and having done all, to stand. Stand therefore, having your loins girt about with truth, and having on the breastplate of righteousness; And your feet shod with the preparation of the gospel of peace; Above all, taking the shield of faith, wherewith ye shall be able to quench all the fiery darts of the wicked. And take the helmet of salvation, and the sword of the Spirit, which is the word of God *(Ephesians 6:11-17)*.

For this purpose the Son of God was manifested, that he might destroy the works of the devil *(I John 3:8)*.

When the enemy shall come in like a flood, the Spirit of the Lord shall lift up a standard against him *(Isaiah 59:19)*.

Greater is he that is in you, than he that is in the world *(I John 4:4)*.

For whatsoever is born of God overcometh the world: and this is the victory that overcometh the world, even our faith *(I John 5:4)*.

But they that wait upon the Lord shall renew their strength; they shall mount up with wings as eagles; they shall run, and not be weary; and they shall walk, and not faint *(Isaiah 40:31)*.

When thou passest through the waters, I will be with thee; and through the rivers, they shall not overflow thee: when thou walkest through the fire, thou shalt not be burned; neither shall the flame kindle upon thee *(Isaiah 43:2)*.

These things I have spoken unto you, that in me ye might have peace. In the world ye shall have tribulation: but be of good cheer; I have overcome the world *(John 16:33)*.

The angel of the Lord encampeth round about them that fear him, and delivereth them *(Psalm 34:7)*.

Verily I say unto you, Whatsoever ye shall bind on earth shall be bound in heaven: and whatsoever ye shall loose on earth shall be loosed in heaven *(Matthew 18:18)*.

And they overcame him [Satan] by the blood of the Lamb [Jesus], and by the word of their testimony . . . *(Revelation 12:11)*.

Submit yourselves therefore to God. Resist the devil, and he will flee from you *(James 4:7)*.

And the God of peace shall bruise Satan under your feet shortly *(Romans 16:20)*.

Through God we shall do valiantly: for he it is that shall tread down our enemies *(Psalm 108:13)*.

Now thanks be unto God, which always causeth us to

triumph in Christ *(II Corinthians 2:14).*

Now unto him that is able to keep you from falling, and to present you faultless before the presence of his glory with exceeding joy, To the only wise God our Saviour, be glory . . . *(Jude 24,25).*

Where the Spirit of the Lord is, there is liberty *(II Corinthians 3:17).*

Stand fast therefore in the liberty wherewith Christ hath made us free, and be not entangled again with the yoke of bondage *(Galatians 5:1).*

Because thou hast made the Lord, which is my refuge, even the most High, they habitation; There shall no evil befall thee, neither shall any plague come nigh thy dwelling *(Psalm 91:9,10).*

Because he hath set his love upon me, therefore will I deliver him: I will set him on high, because he hath known my name. He shall call upon me, and I will answer him: I will be with him in trouble; I will deliver him, and honour him *(Psalm 91:14,15).*

No weapon that is formed against thee shall prosper; and every tongue that shall rise against thee in judgment thou shalt condemn. This is the heritage of the servants of the Lord, and their righteousness is of me, saith the Lord *(Isaiah 54:17).*

He delivereth me from mine enemies: yea, thou liftest me up above those that rise up against me: thou hast delivered me from the violent man *(Psalm 18:48).*

Behold, I give unto you power to tread on serpents and scorpions, and over all the power of the enemy: and nothing shall by any means hurt you *(Luke 10:19)*.

He that dwelleth in the secret place of the most High shall abide under the shadow of the Almighty *(Psalm 91:1)*.

He shall cover thee with his feathers, and under his wings shalt thou trust. . . *(Psalm 91:4)*.

A thousand shall fall at thy side, and ten thousand at thy right hand; but it shall not come nigh thee *(Psalm 91:7)*.

Nay, in all these things we are more than conquerors through him that loved us *(Romans 8:37)*.

10
God's Promises Concerning Abundant Life

God does not expect you to be needy or in want. *The Lord is my shepherd; I SHALL NOT WANT.* His Rainbow of Promises assures us that *God shall supply all your need according to His riches in glory,* but God's help is conditional. What are the conditions? *Seek ye first the Kingdom of God and His righteousness; and all these things shall be added unto you* (Matthew 6:33). In this verse Jesus is telling you how to receive from God, how He will take care of you who are obedient and put Him first in your lives. Reach into His Rainbow of Promises in faith believing, and you will have the abundance of God.

I am come that they might have life, and that they might have it more abundantly *(John 10:10)*.

And we know that all things work together for good to them that love God, to them who are the called according to his purpose *(Romans 8:28)*.

Ye have not chosen me, but I have chosen you, and ordained you, that ye should go and bring forth fruit, and that your fruit should remain: that whatsoever ye shall ask of the Father in my name, he may give it you *(John 15:16)*.

If ye abide in me, and my words abide in you, ye shall ask what ye will, and it shall be done unto you. Herein is my Father glorified, that ye bear much fruit . . . *(John 15:7,8)*.

They that seek the Lord shall not want any good thing *(Psalm 34:10)*.

Every good gift and every perfect gift is from above, and cometh down from the Father . . . *(James 1:17)*.

[The Lord] who satisfieth thy mouth with good things; so that thy youth is renewed like the eagle's *(Psalm 103:5)*.

This book of the law shall not depart out of thy mouth . . . for then thou shalt make thy way prosperous, and then thou shalt have good success *(Joshua 1:8)*.

Then shalt thou prosper, if thou takest heed to fulfill the statutes and judgments which the Lord charged

Moses with concerning Israel: be strong, and of good courage; dread not, nor be dismayed *(I Chronicles 22:13).*

As long as he sought the Lord, God made him to prosper *(II Chronicles 26:5).*

I am the Lord thy God, which brought thee out of the land of Egypt: open thy mouth wide, and I will fill it *(Psalm 81:10).*

The righteous shall flourish like the palm tree *(Psalm 92:12).*

But my God shall supply all your need according to his riches in glory by Christ Jesus *(Philippians 4:19).*

But as it is written, Eye hath not seen, nor ear heard, neither have entered into the heart of man, the things which God hath prepared for them that love him *(I Corinthians 2:9).*

For the Lord God is a sun and shield: the Lord will give grace and glory: no good thing will he withhold from them that walk uprightly *(Psalm 84:11).*

And to know the love of Christ, which passeth knowledge, that ye might be filled with all the fullness of God *(Ephesians 3:19).*

But the fruit of the Spirit is love, joy, peace, longsuffering, gentleness, goodness, faith, Meekness, temperance . . . *(Galatians 5:22,23).*

The blessing of the Lord, it maketh rich, and he addeth no sorrow with it *(Proverbs 10:22).*

And God is able to make all grace abound toward you; that ye, always having all sufficiency in all things, may abound to every good work *(II Corinthians 9:8).*

And every one that hath forsaken houses, or brethren, or sisters, or father, or mother, or wife, or children, or lands, for my name's sake, shall receive an hundredfold, and shall inherit everlasting life*(Matthew 19:29).*

He that spared not his own Son, but delivered him up for us all, how shall he not with him also freely give us all things *(Romans 8:32)?*

They shall be abundantly satisfied with the fatness of thy house; and thou shalt make them drink of the river of thy pleasures *(Psalm 36:8).*

Now unto him that is able to do exceeding abundantly above all that we ask or think, according to the power that worketh in us *(Ephesians 3:20).*

And your threshing shall reach unto the vintage, and the vintage shall reach unto the sowing time: and ye shall eat your bread to the full, and dwell in your land safely *(Leviticus 26:5).*

O love the Lord, all ye his saints: for the Lord preserveth the faithful, and plentifully rewardeth the proud doer *(Psalm 31:23).*

But whoso hearkeneth unto me shall dwell safely, and

shall be quiet from fear of evil *(Proverbs 1:33).*

Trust in the Lord, and do good; so shalt thou dwell in the land, and verily thou shalt be fed. Delight thyself also in the Lord; and he shall give thee the desires of thine heart *(Psalm 37:3,4).*

11
God's Promises Concerning Financial and Material Blessings

The plan of receiving by giving is in God's Rainbow of Promises. The Lord will give to you if you give to Him, but by your not giving you can expect nothing back. In the book of Malachi, God accuses the Israelites of robbing Him of tithes and offerings. God had promised to open up the heavens and pour out a blessing on His people, but it was conditioned upon their paying God ten percent of their income and giving beyond that in love offerings. The plan of tithing was in effect before the law was given, was in effect in New Testament times and is still a part of God's Rainbow of Promises today. If you expect God to move for you, you must be obedient to Him in all things.

Beloved, I wish above all things that thou mayest prosper . . . even as thy soul prospereth *(III John 2)*.

Your Father knoweth what things ye have need of, before ye ask him . . . But seek ye first the kingdom of God, and his righteousness; and all these things shall be added unto you *(Matthew 6:8,33)*.

Bring ye all the tithes into the storehouse, that there may be meat in mine house, and prove me now herewith, saith the Lord of hosts, if I will not open you the windows of heaven, and pour you out a blessing, that there shall not be room enough to receive it *(Malachi 3:10)*.

But this I say, He which soweth sparingly shall reap also sparingly; and he which soweth bountifully shall reap also bountifully. Every man according as he purposeth in his heart, so let him give; not grudgingly, or of necessity: for God loveth a cheerful giver. And God is able to make all grace abound toward you; that ye, always having all sufficiency in all things, may abound to every good work *(II Corinthians 9:6-8)*.

Upon the first day of the week let every one of you lay by him in store, as God hath prospered him . . . *(I Corinthians 16:2)*.

Our sufficiency is of God *(II Corinthians 3:5)*.

Charge them that are rich in this world, that they be not high minded, nor trust in uncertain riches, but in the living God, who giveth us richly all things to enjoy *(I Timothy 6:17)*.

The Lord is my shepherd; I shall not want *(Psalm 23:1)*.

Therefore I say unto you, Take no thought for your life, what ye shall eat, or what ye shall drink; nor yet for your body, what ye shall put on . . . Wherefore, if God so clothe the grass of the field, which to-day is, and to-morrow is cast into the oven, shall he not much more clothe you, O ye of little faith*(Matthew 6:25,30)?*

Trust in the Lord, and do good; so shalt thou dwell in the land, and verily thou shalt be fed *(Psalm 37:3)*.

Give, and it shall be given unto you; good measure, pressed down, and shaken together, and running over, shall men give into your bosom . . . *(Luke 6:38)*.

Honour the Lord with thy substance, and with the firstfruits of all thine increase: So shall thy barns be filled with plenty, and thy presses shall burst out with new wine *(Proverbs 3:9,10)*.

If ye be willing and obedient, ye shall eat the good of the land *(Isaiah 1:19)*.

I have been young, and now am old; yet have I not seen the righteous forsaken, nor his seed begging bread *(Psalm 37:25)*.

Since the people began to bring the offerings into the house of the Lord we have had enough to eat, and have left plenty: for the Lord hath blessed his people; and that which is left is this great store *(II Chronicles 31:10)*.

If thou wert pure and upright; surely now he would awake for thee, and make the habitation of thy righteousness prosperous *(Job 8:6).*

O fear the Lord, ye his saints: for there is no want to them that fear him. The young lions do lack, and suffer hunger: but they that seek the Lord shall not want any good thing *(Psalm 34:9,10).*

In the house of the righteous is much treasure: but in the revenues of the wicked is trouble *(Proverbs 15:6).*

The upright shall have good things in possession *(Proverbs 28:10).*

That I may cause those that love me to inherit substance; and I will fill their treasures *(Proverbs 8:21).*

For every beast of the forest is mine, and the cattle upon a thousand hills *(Psalm 50:10).*

Every man also to whom God hath given riches and wealth, and hath given him power to eat thereof, and to take his portion, and to rejoice in his labour; this is the gift of God *(Ecclesiastes 5:19).*

And the Lord thy God will make thee plenteous in every work of thine hand, in the fruit of thy body, and in the fruit of thy cattle, and in the fruit of thy land, for good . . . *(Deuteronomy 30:9).*

12

God's Promises Concerning Guidance and a Plain Path

Who and what are you? Where are you going? Is your life structured around God's Rainbow of Promises which tells you that you will not get to heaven by works, but through the blood of Christ? The Word of God will never change; and to reap all its benefits, to walk God's plain path, you must claim all of God's promises. Let Jesus breathe His breath of life into you as you accept His marvelous guidance.

Trust in the Lord with all thine heart; and lean not unto thine own understanding. In all thy ways acknowledge him, and he shall direct thy paths *(Proverbs 3:5,6).*

Thy word is a lamp unto my feet, and a light unto my path *(Psalm 119:105).*

If any of you lack wisdom, let him ask of God, that giveth to all men liberally, and upbraideth not; and it shall be given him *(James 1:5).*

I will instruct thee and teach thee in the way which thou shalt go: I will guide thee with mine eye *(Psalm 32:8).*

And thine ears shall hear a word behind thee, saying, This is the way, walk ye in it, when ye turn to the right hand, and when ye turn to the left *(Isaiah 30:21).*

Teach me thy way, O Lord, and lead me in a plain path, because of mine enemies *(Psalm 27:11).*

He shall feed his flock like a shepherd: he shall gather the lambs with his arm, and carry them in his bosom, and shall gently lead those that are with young *(Isaiah 40:11).*

And he [the Lord] said, My presence shall go with thee *(Exodus 33:14).*

But the anointing which ye have received of him abideth in you, and ye need not that any man teach you: but as the same anointing teacheth you of all things, and is truth, and is no lie, and even as it hath taught you, ye shall abide in him *(I John 2:27).*

Let this mind be in you, which was also in Christ Jesus *(Philippians 2:5).*

We have the mind of Christ *(I Corinthians 2:16).*

He leadeth me beside the still waters *(Psalm 23:2).*

For thou art my lamp, O Lord: and the Lord will lighten my darkness . . . God is my strength and power: And he maketh my way perfect *(II Samuel 22:29,33).*

But when they deliver you up, take no thought how or what ye shall speak: for it shall be given you in that same hour what ye shall speak. For it is not ye that speak, but the Spirit of your Father which speaketh in you *(Matthew 10:19,20).*

Whosoever believeth on me should not abide in darkness *(John 12:46).*

This I say then, Walk in the Spirit, and ye shall not fulfill the lust of the flesh *(Galatians 5:16).*

The meek will he guide in judgment: and the meek will he teach his way *(Psalm 25:9).*

For this God is our God for ever and ever: he will be our guide even unto death *(Psalm 48:14).*

Thou shalt guide me with thy counsel, and afterward

receive me to glory *(Psalm 73:24).*

And I will bring the blind by a way that they knew not; I will lead them in paths that they have not known: I will make darkness light before them, and crooked things straight. These things will I do unto them, and not forsake them *(Isaiah 42:16).*

To give light to them that sit in darkness and in the shadow of death, to guide our feet into the way of peace *(Luke 1:79).*

Search me, O God, and know my heart: try me, and know my thoughts: And see if there be any wicked way in me, and lead me in the way everlasting *(Psalm 139:23,24).*

13
God's Promises Concerning Help in Time of Need

The three Hebrew boys didn't bow and they didn't burn in the fiery furnace—they had confidence in their Rainbow of Promises. Daniel was saved from the jaws of the lions because he had a Rainbow of Promises from God. The fiery furnaces, the lions' dens of your life lose their threats when you act on all of God's Word. Why be tormented, devastated and in despair when you can be a whole person in Christ Jesus no matter how difficult your circumstances? Jesus will always stand by His Rainbow of Promises.

And we know that all things work together for good to them that love God, to them who are the called according to his purpose *(Romans 8:28)*.

There hath no temptation taken you but such as is common to man: but God is faithful, who will not suffer you to be tempted above that ye are able; but will with the temptation also make a way to escape, that ye may be able to bear it *(I Corinthians 10:13)*.

For he hath said, I will never leave thee, nor forsake thee. So that we may boldly say, The Lord is my helper, and I will not fear what man shall do unto me *(Hebrews 13:5,6)*.

Are not two sparrows sold for a farthing? and one of them shall not fall on the ground without your Father. But the very hairs of your head are all numbered. Fear ye not therefore, ye are of more value than many sparrows *(Matthew 10:29-31)*.

Yea, though I walk through the valley of the shadow of death, I will fear no evil: for thou art with me; thy rod and thy staff they comfort me. Thou preparest a table before me in the presence of mine enemies: thou anointest my head with oil; my cup runneth over *(Psalm 23:4,5)*.

Casting all your care upon him; for he careth for you *(I Peter 5:7)*.

For God hath not given us the spirit of fear; but of power, and of love, and of a sound mind *(II Timothy 1:7)*.

Peace I leave with you, my peace I give unto you: not as the world giveth, give I unto you. Let not your heart be troubled, neither let it be afraid *(John 14:27)*.

But they that wait upon the Lord shall renew their strength; they shall mount up with wings as eagles; they shall run, and not be weary; and they shall walk, and not faint *(Isaiah 40:31)*.

I called upon the Lord in distress: The Lord answered me, and set me in a large place. The Lord is on my side; I will not fear: what can man do unto me *(Psalm 118:5,6)?*

Let us therefore come boldly unto the throne of grace, that we may obtain mercy, and find grace to help in time of need *(Hebrews 4:16)*.

Blessed are they that mourn: for they shall be comforted *(Matthew 5:4)*.

Come unto me, all ye that labour and are heavy laden, and I will give you rest. Take my yoke upon you, and learn of me; for I am meek and lowly in heart: and ye shall find rest unto your souls. For my yoke is easy, and my burden is light *(Matthew 11:28-30)*.

For the Lord God will help me; therefore shall I not be confounded: therefore have I set my face like a flint, and I know that I shall not be ashamed *(Isaiah 50:7)*.

For I am persuaded, that neither death, nor life, nor angels, nor principalities, nor powers, nor things present, nor things to come, Nor height, nor depth, nor any other creature, shall be able to separate us from the love of God, which is in Christ Jesus our Lord *(Romans 8:38,39)*.

Beloved, think it not strange concerning the fiery trial which is to try you, as though some strange thing happened unto you: But rejoice, inasmuch as ye are partakers of Christ's sufferings . . . *(I Peter 4:12,13)*.

In his favor is life: weeping may endure for a night, but joy cometh in the morning *(Psalm 30:5)*.

My help cometh from the Lord, which made heaven and earth. He will not suffer thy foot to be moved: he that keepeth thee will not slumber . . . The Lord shall preserve thee from all evil: he shall preserve thy soul *(Psalm 121:2,3,7)*.

Fear thou not; for I am with thee: be not dismayed; for I am thy God: I will strengthen thee; yea, I will help thee; yea, I will uphold thee with the right hand of my righteousness *(Isaiah 41:10)*.

If I take the wings of the morning, and dwell in the uttermost parts of the sea; Even there shall thy hand lead me, and thy right hand shall hold me *(Psalm 139:9,10)*.

Thy right hand hath holden me up, and thy gentleness hath made me great *(Psalm 18:35)*.

Wherefore let them that suffer according to the will of God commit the keeping of their souls to him in well-doing, as unto a faithful Creator *(I Peter 4:19)*.

The Lord will strengthen him upon the bed of languishing: thou wilt make all his bed in his sickness *(Psalm 41:3)*.

Trust in the Lord, and do good; so shalt thou dwell in the land, and verily thou shalt be fed *(Psalm 37:3)*.

For thou hast been a strength to the poor, a strength to the needy in his distress, a refuge from the storm, a shadow from the heat, when the blast of the terrible ones is as a storm against the wall *(Isaiah 25:4)*.

They that sow in tears shall reap in joy. He that goeth forth and weepeth, bearing precious seed, shall doubtless come again with rejoicing, bringing his sheaves with him *(Psalm 126:5,6)*.

God setteth the solitary in families: he bringeth out those which are bound with chains *(Psalm 68:6)*.

I can do all things through Christ which strengtheneth me *(Philippians 4:13)*.

The Lord knoweth how to deliver the godly out of temptations *(II Peter 2:9)*.

Be strengthened with might by his Spirit in the inner man *(Ephesians 3:16)*.

Be of good courage, and he shall strengthen your heart, all ye that hope in the Lord *(Psalm 31:24)*.

Mine eyes are ever toward the Lord; for he shall pluck my feet out of the net *(Psalm 25:15)*.

Cast thy burden upon the Lord, and he shall sustain thee: he shall never suffer the righteous to be moved *(Psalm 55:22)*.

My grace is sufficient for thee: for my strength is made perfect in weakness *(II Corinthians 12:9)*.

Many are the afflictions of the righteous: but the Lord delivereth him out of them all *(Psalm 34:19)*.

For in that he himself hath suffered being tempted, he is able to succour them that are tempted *(Hebrews 2:18)*.

Blessed is the man that endureth temptation: for when he is tried, he shall receive the crown of life, which the Lord hath promised to them that love him *(James 1:12)*.

The Lord is nigh unto them that are of a broken heart; and saveth such as be of a contrite spirit *(Psalm 34:18)*.

God is our refuge and strength, a very present help in trouble *(Psalm 46:1)*.

For thou hast delivered my soul from death, mine eyes from tears, and my feet from falling *(Psalm 116:8)*.

What time I am afraid, I will trust in thee *(Psalm 56:3)*.

But whoso hearkeneth unto me shall dwell safely, and shall be quiet from fear of evil *(Proverbs 1:33)*.

I sought the Lord, and he heard me, and delivered me from all my fears *(Psalm 34:4)*.

He [the upright] shall not be afraid of evil tidings: his heart is fixed, trusting in the Lord *(Psalm 112:7)*.

There is no fear in love; but perfect love casteth out fear *(I John 4:18)*.

Thou wilt keep him in perfect peace, whose mind is stayed on thee: because he trusteth in thee *(Isaiah 26:3)*.

Be not afraid of sudden fear, neither of the desolation of the wicked, when it cometh. For the Lord shall be thy confidence, and shall keep thy foot from being taken *(Proverbs 3:25,26)*.

Lo, I am with you alway, even unto the end of the world *(Matthew 28:20)*.

The Lord is good, a strong hold in the day of trouble; and he knoweth them that trust in him *(Nahum 1:7)*.

He will regard the prayer of the destitute, and not despise their prayer *(Psalm 102:17)*.

I know whom I have believed, and am persuaded that he is able to keep that which I have committed unto him *(II Timothy 1:12)*.

Be careful for nothing; but in every thing by prayer and supplication with thanksgiving let your requests be made known unto God. And the peace of God, which passeth all understanding, shall keep your hearts and minds through Christ Jesus *(Philippians 4:6,7)*.

For as the sufferings of Christ abound in us, so our consolation also aboundeth by Christ... that as ye are partakers of the sufferings, so shall ye be also of the consolation *(II Corinthians 1:5,7)*.

A Final Word of Encouragement

Doubt and fear that the Lord will not do what He has said will block you from receiving all the abundance of God's Rainbow of Promises. What is in His Rainbow of Promises? Healing for soul, mind and body, love to sustain and take you through the deepest valleys. Eternal life in the riches of glory—all are promised to the Children of God who love Him and put Him first in their lives.

You can meet the conditions of receiving these promises through walking by faith, not by feelings; for in the feeling realm the enemy can most easily deceive and rob you. Faith, believing that God is God and He will do for you what He has promised regardless of how you feel about it, is in His Rainbow of Promises. Decide that you have a contract with God—it is one He never will break. Have faith in the promise of a glorified body given to those taken alive in the Rapture—and to the dead in Christ: a new body to come forth from the grave, a body not subject to death, pain or disease. God's Rainbow of Promises is fantastic indeed; its conditions are well worth meeting so you can be made whole, delivered; but if you doubt, you need not think you will receive.

Take God's Rainbow of Promises; abide by it. Meet the conditions with unwavering faith and you will be eligible for a miracle. Having heard all that God has made available to us in His great Rainbow of Promises, it's time to act upon it, time to rise up and possess the land. Serve the Lord with a perfect heart full of love, and He will move for you.

About the Author

Reverend Ernest Angley, pastor and founder of Ernest Angley's Grace Cathedral in Akron Ohio, is in the midst of a tremendous worldwide outreach ministry, spreading the Gospel by way of crusades, television and the printed page into 166 nations at the time of this writing. God has endowed Reverend Angley with special gifts to bring healing for soul, mind and body to the multitudes. He does not claim to be a healer, but a witness to the marvelous healing power of Christ. His television programs, "The Ernest Angley Hour" (aired weekly) and "The Ninety and Nine Club" (aired daily), present the fullness of God's Word to the people—salvation, healing and the baptism in the Holy Ghost.

Check your local listing for times in your area.

Ernest Angley's Grace Cathedral
Akron, Ohio

MORE BOOKS
by Ernest Angley

FAITH IN GOD HEALS THE SICK $1.95
An instructive book by Ernest Angley telling not only how to receive physical healing from the Lord, but also how to keep that healing.

UNTYING GOD'S HANDS $2.95
With amazing frankness the author has dealt with many controversial subjects in this book: the ministry of angels, preparation required for the Rapture, guidelines for dating, sex in marriage, sex outside marriage, masturbation, homosexuality. Many other subjects covering the whole life of man are woven into the underlying theme of how to untie God's hands.

CELL 15 $2.95
The dramatic true story of the imprisonment of Reverend Ernest Angley in Munich, Germany, for preaching the Gospel and praying for the sick.